Frank Noë

Amsterdam Cook Book

Traditional food, recipes and stories of Holland's capital

UITGEVERIJ
Het Zwarte Schaap

CONTENTS

MAKING DO WITH LITTLE

It is pretty hard to say what made up the diet of 'ordinary' Amsterdam folk through the ages. Fish must have featured prominently on the daily menu, particularly in the city's first few centuries, when it was still a fishing village. It was in the fifteenth and sixteenth centuries that this little village became a major town. At this stage, Amsterdam had gained major prominence as a transhipment port in international trade, which was burgeoning. So much grain (wheat and rye) was landed here from the Baltic that one could call the city 'Europe's granary'. So, it's no surprise that, at that time, bread and other grain products (gruel, pancakes and the like) were Amsterdam's staples. Anyone who could afford it supplemented their diet with some vegetables or boiled meat, which was served up as something between a thick soup and a stew (but there were no potatoes in it; these hadn't been brought to Europe yet). A lot of watery beer was drunk, because the water from the city's canals was too filthy to consume. Another drink, which rapidly became widespread, was jenever. Gin, like beer, is grain-based, after all.

In the mid-seventeenth century, the American potato reached the Low Countries, though it didn't catch on for quite a while.. Until quite late into the eighteenth century, potatoes were mainly served to pigs and prisoners. However, after 1800, it became the main source of nutrition for the masses. Fresh meat and vegetables remained unaffordable for most people. Even in the nineteenth century, concerns were building about the need for a varied diet, so people were encouraged to make a simple soup: for example, one based on water, barley, salt, pepper, potatoes and a few vegetables. The main sustenance apart from potatoes in this era was gruel and pancakes.

Potatoes kept their prime position in the Dutch diet in the twentieth century. This was seen clearly enough in the Potato Riots that broke out in Amsterdam in 1917 (see p. 64).

A vegetable soup recipe given in a cookery school magazine of that year, distributed to practical schools for girls, shows well enough that the Dutch, although neutral, had to make do with very little during the First World War. We can surmise from it that even stock cubes were still an unaffordable luxury for many.

Up-to-date vegetable soup

2 l water
4 small leeks
1 bunch of celery
1 floret of cauliflower
2 small carrots or turnips
1 kg potatoes

We can't get hold of meat, fat, vermicelli or rice any more, so well have to do without.
Lets make a soup of what's left: a good range of vegetables, potatoes, water and salt. Those whose budget permits can add in one or more stock cubes, but this is not necessary. As long as the soup is made well, and one is sensible enough not to dwell on whats not in it while one eats, then even these pared-down soups will do for children and unpretentious adults.

Next page: *Oudekerksplein 50, c. 1910. Three women chatting in front of Café Het Zwaantje, the woman on the right is holding a loaf.* ▸

Bread

RYE BREAD, WHITE BREAD, BROWN BREAD

Historians estimate that the baking trade was fully-developed in Amsterdam from the early fourteenth century onwards. At first, the bakers got their grain from Zeeland and the eastern Netherlands; but, from the mid-fourteenth century onwards, Baltic grain cornered the market. Rye represented the bulk of imports, as it was cheaper than wheat. Something else that came to Amsterdam around 1300 was the first grain mill, which indicates two things: baking was increasingly professional, and there was great demand for flour. The bakers brought their own sacks of grain to the mill for grinding by the miller.

It was a tough life for bakers and their assistants: they had to do their baking at night, do their delivery rounds in the morning and bake cakes and biscuits for the rest of the day.

Factory bakeries arose in the nineteenth century. The celebrated Amsterdam doctor Samuel Sarphati – after whom a street is named to this day – set up the first bakery of this sort in 1856. This manufacturing method resulted in a cheaper price per loaf. For centuries what people meant by 'bread' was rye bread. As it was cheap, it was the bread of the masses. White bread, made of wheat, was a luxury. It was only in the twentieth century that the working class was able to afford it occasionally. Brown (wholemeal) bread was initially regarded as a poor man's loaf, but this changed in the late nineteenth century. The British doctor Thomas Allinson – still known for his 'Allinson loaf' – urged that people eat brown bread, and particularly wholemeal bread, with no part of the grain discarded. In Amsterdam, two socialist-minded brothers answered his call: in 1892, they opened a brown loaf bakery on the corner of Ceintuurbaan and Ferdinand Bolstraat. There is still a bakery on that corner today. This changed the poor image of brown bread in Amsterdam.

Seller of loaves, cakes and biscuits

HALF-AND-HALF SANDWICH

Broodje halfom • [ˈbrocə ˈhɑlfɔm]

Makes 1 sandwich

A broodje halfom *is the simplest, and also the most classic, Amsterdam item in the city's culinary repertoire.*
Amsterdam, home to half of all Dutch Jews before the Second World War, has a myriad of Jewish influences. We will continue to come across them throughout this book. Jewish cooking is one of those influences. Traditional Jewish cuisine involves a strict separation of meat from dairy products (so they are never served at the same meal). This is such a strict separation that Orthodox families maintain two worktops and two sets of crockery and cutlery in the kitchen, and sometimes even two dishwashers. So, understandably the butter in the below recipe makes this the non-kosher variant.
A broodje halfom (half liver, salt cured meat) has been standard fare at Amsterdam coffee houses since the mid-nineteenth century.

Ingredients

1 white roll
butter for buttering (as desired)
2 slices of boiled beef liver
2 slices of salt cured beef or pastrami
salt and freshly-ground pepper

Cut the roll open and butter both sides.
Cover the bottom of it with the cured beef and liver.
Sprinkle salt and pepper on the liver and close the roll.

For a more upmarket version

The above ingredients, plus
a handful of lettuce
¼ red onion, sliced
1 pickled gherkin, sliced

Place the lettuce and meats on the sandwich, garnish it with onion and a gherkin, and fold it closed.

ROAD WORKERS ROLL

Stratenmakertje • [ˈstratenˈmakərcə]

Makes 10 sandwiches

Sal Santen (1915-1988), a Dutch Jewish writer, wrote about the stratenmakertje in his memoirs. 'At lunchtimes, Maup and I eat in Van der Helst Street. We always order a stratenmakertje, half a loaf cut in half lengthwise. It's easier than a regular sandwich and a lot tastier.'
If there were several eaters, the whole or half loaf could also be sliced vertically. The filling could, of course, be anything. Poverty will have played a role in this variant, which consists of more bread than filling.
Here's an up-to-date version.

Ingredients

10 slices puff pastry
200 g grated cheese (Gouda or Edam)
3 tbsp sour cream
1 tsp coarsely-ground pepper
1 egg, whisked
½ cucumber
2 tomatoes
salt and freshly-ground pepper
5 slices ham
5 slices cheese

Let the pastry sheets thaw for about 10 minutes.
Preheat the oven to 200 °C.
Mix the grated cheese with the sour cream and pepper.
Lay a sheet of baking paper on the tray and place the pastry sheets on it.
Glaze them with whisked egg and spread the cheese mix evenly over the sheets.
Bake them golden brown for about 10 minutes.
Thinly slice the cucumber and tomatoes and sprinkle salt and pepper on them.
Cut the ham and cheese slices in half diagonally.
After baking, cut the pastry sheets open horizontally and fill them, sandwich-like, with the ham, cheese, cucumber and tomato.

AMSTERDAM SANDWICH

Broodje Mokum • [ˈbrocə ˈmokəm]

Makes 1 sandwich

A broodje Mokum *is more than just a sandwich with authentic Amsterdam ingredients; it's also the name of a well-known Amsterdam coffee house.*

A koffiehuis *(not to be confused with a coffeeshop, which is a soft drugs pub) is a slightly old-fashioned Dutch word for the older kind of lunchroom. In fact, even the English loanword 'lunchroom' is a bit old-fashioned nowadays. These are catering establishments that mainly serve coffee, milk and buttermilk, and straightforward sandwiches. They were not typically noted for their convivial atmosphere; the usual decor was fluorescent tubes and tiled walls. In Dutch usage, the word café suggests a touch more class, which is something you couldn't say of an old koffiehuis with its formica-topped tables, plastic checked tablecloths and endless signs with 'Coffee's ready'.*

Ingredients

1 white bap or roll*
50 g beef sausage (ossenworst), sliced
50 g mature cheese, sliced
butter for buttering
a few Amsterdam onions
mustard to taste

Halve the bread through the middle lengthways and butter both sides.
Cover the bottom slice with the sausage and cheese.
Place the onions on top of that and close the sandwich.
The sausage and cheese can be seasoned to taste with mustard.

* Preferably of the moist white variety

tip Try using onion chips and/or gherkin slices instead of the Amsterdam onions.

Teetotallers' coffee house on the Singel, c. 1910

GEHEEL ONTHOUDERS KOFFIEHUIS
BURGER-HOTEL
BURGER HOTEL
BURGER HOTEL
EXPEDITIE NAARDEN HUIZEN SASSENHEIM LISSE ALKMAAR OOSTERHOUT.
GEEN VERKOOP PER GLAS

DUIVEKATER HOLIDAY LOAF

Duivekater • [ˈdœyfəˈkatər]

Makes two loaves

Duivekater is a sweetened bread enjoyed in and around Amsterdam in the sixteenth and seventeenth centuries on the December festival days: Sinterklaas, Christmas and New Year's Eve. It was also served at Easter and Pentecost. With a little imagination, you can see its resemblance to a shinbone: it's a long, thin loaf with a bulb at each end. It may be the vestige of an old pagan ritual: originally, animals were sacrificed, and later they came to be symbolised by offering up a tibia-shaped loaf. That would explain why the loaf is also known as scheengebak, 'shin-cake'. Some Jan Steen paintings portray duivekaters. To this day, there are a few pockets of the Netherlands where duivekaters are still baked.

Ingredients

500 g flour
5 g salt
30 g yeast
200 cl milk, lukewarm
50 g butter, melted
100 g sugar
juice of half a lemon
1 egg, beaten

Preheat the oven to 200 °C. Place the flour in a mixing bowl, add salt and make an indentation in the middle.
Dissolve the yeast in the milk and pour it into the indentation. Then add the butter (melted), sugar and lemon juice and mix it all throughout the mixture from the middle outwards.
Then, knead the clump into a supple dough and let it rise for an hour on a lukewarm, damp tray. After that, make two lumps out of it and let them rise for a further 15 minutes.
Then fold the lumps to make long loaves, tapered at both ends. Let them rise for a further 15 minutes on a greased baking tray. Shorten both ends once with scissors and curl the trimmed-off points back towards the middle. Using a knife, carve figures or geometric patterns on the top of the loaves and glaze them with a beaten egg. Bake them for 35 to 40 minutes in the preheated oven, until they are brown and done.

Jan Steen painting: Baker with duivekater (festival loaf)

HOW AMSTERDAM GOT ITS NICKNAME 'MOKUM'

We'll be seeing throughout this book that Amsterdam's Jewish residents have influenced it in many areas of life. This even extends to the name '*Mokum*', which comes from Hebrew *maqom*, meaning 'place' or 'city'. This became mokem in Yiddish, a Germanic language written in the Hebrew alphabet. In time, this became bastardised to 'Mokum'. From the late sixteenth century onwards, Amsterdam was a city of refuge for Jews facing persecution in Southern, Central and Eastern Europe. Here, they were welcome (or, more strictly speaking, tolerated), and they could retain their religion and identity more or less intact. About half of all Dutch Jews lived in Amsterdam until the Second World War.

In Dutch Jewish usage, cities were often referred to simply by a letter of the Hebrew alphabet. Amsterdam was *Mokum Aleph* ('City A'); Delft, *Mokum Dalet* ('City D'). Later, this custom fell into disuse, leaving just the word *Mokum* denoting Amsterdam. It is said this was retained in gratitude for the extended hospitality that the Jewish population enjoyed in the city.

Some Yiddish words found their way into *Bargoens*, an underworld jargon of the early twentieth century. It was the slang used by people on the margins of society: the homeless, market traders, fairgoers and *penoze* (another Yiddish loanword, meaning 'gangland').

Amsterdam's old city crest, featuring a cog ship. Munttoren ▸

MISS WANNÉE AND THE AMSTERDAMSCHE HUISHOUDSCHOOL COOKBOOK

One could hardly write an Amsterdam cookbook without mentioning Cornelia Johanna Wannée (1880-1932). She was a Rotterdammer by birth but moved with her family to Amsterdam at the age of seventeen. After high school, she was employed teaching at a *huishoudschool*, a girls' practical school. In 1904, she became the cookery and diet teacher at the *Amsterdamsche Huishoudschool.* Six years later, she published her *Kookboek van de Amsterdamsche Huishoudschool*, a book of recipes taught at the school. More than a century on, the book is still in print today. A fundamental distinction made in this cookbook is between burgerkeuken or 'citizens' cuisine', which Miss Wannée taught should be tasty but nutritious and economical, and *fijne keuken*, 'fine cuisine', with more chic dishes. One of the titles with which her book was in competition was the already-successful *Recepten van de Haagsche Kookschool*, a Hague equivalent also based on recipes taught at a school. But Miss Wannée's attitude, which managed to be both simple and refined, meant that her book sold like hotcakes. It was largely her publisher, Becht, which benefited, as they had agreed the fixed fee of four hundred guilders with the authoress and also contractually obliged her to follow up with another cookbook. Miss Wannée died a spinster in 1932, aged 52. The book has been through countless reprints and revisions since. More than a million copies have been sold and it's not too much of a stretch to say that no Dutch household is complete without it. Some cookery writers were sworn enemies of the *huishoudschool* model of cooking, because these schools taught their girls to be parsimonious with ingredients.

The Amsterdamsche Huishoudschool (cooking school for girls) on Zandpad ▸

AMSTERDAMSCH
HUISHOUDSCHOOL

Warm dishes

AMSTERDAM MEATBALL

Amsterdamse gehaktbal • ['æmstədæmsə' xə'haktbal]

Serves 4-6

Until the late fifties, Jordaan, the much-celebrated and over-romanticised working-class neighbourhood in west-central Amsterdam, was in reality an impoverished and fairly miserable place, with profound unemployment along with housing and social issues. One of the ways that housewives supplemented meagre incomes here was shrimp peeling. This was really a women's speciality and grandmothers, mothers and granddaughters teamed up with their neighbours to take on the task. They peeled the shrimp at the dining table, and in the summer sat outside the front door to do it. Shrimp was cheap, meat was expensive; this is why Amsterdammers developed the custom of mixing ground meat with shrimp in their meatballs. Sometimes, the shrimp used for this were the ones that had been crushed in peeling.

Ingredients

1 shallot or small onion, finely diced
75 g butter
1 slice white bread, crusts cut off
dash of milk
400 g mince (half pork, half beef)
salt and pepper
1 egg, beaten
a knife-tip of nutmeg
100 g smallest Dutch shrimps (Hollandse garnalen), peeled

Gently brown the shallot or onion in a knob of butter. Leave to cool. Soak the bread in a dash of milk.

Squeeze it dry, mix it with the mince and the other ingredients, and knead it all together thoroughly. Using dampened hands, make four to six meatballs with the mixture.

Warm the rest of the butter in a frying pan or casserole and fry the meatballs, initially browning them thoroughly at high heat and then leaving them on a lower flame for about 20 minutes until tender. Carefully turn them over from time to time to brown them nicely on all sides.

‘MOKUM *CEMENT*’

Mokums cement • [ˈmokəms səˈmɛnt]

Serves 4

Mash is something found in every era and place. Every country has its own variations. Our method is to boil potatoes, add vegetables (a good way to use up yesterday's leftovers), a bit of liquid or cooking fat, and mash away. The Dutch have tended to add fried bacon rinds and/or smoked sausage when they could afford it. But 'Mokum cement' also goes fantastically with an Amsterdam meatball, of course.

Ingredients

500 g bacon rinds (spekreepjes)
handful of Amsterdam onions
1 kg potatoes
800 g kidney beans (tinned)
optional: milk to taste
pepper

Fry the bacon rinds in a frying pan with no added fat until they have stopped exuding liquid. Remove them from the pan.
Drain the pickled onions and gently fry them in the bacon fat left in the pan until they are shiny.
Peel the potatoes and boil them for approx. 20 minutes until soft.
Heat the kidney beans in their own liquid.
Strain the potatoes and beans and keep some of the cooking liquid handy.
Mash the potatoes, beans and onions together with the frying fat.
Add the rinds.
If necessary for extra softness, add some milk or cooking liquid.
Season with pepper to taste.
Anyone who was still wondering why this dish has been christened 'cement' will see why now: that's just what it looks like.

tip Improved with a dash of mustard.

TURNIP GREENS, APPLE AND BLUE CHEESE

Amsterdams Vet met appel en blauwaderkaas

[æmstəˈdæms vɛt mɛt ˈɑpəl ɛn ˈblɑuwə kas]

Serves 4 as starter or lunch

Despite its Dutch name, Amsterdams Vet *is not the fat in which you fry an Amsterdam meatball. Ask people what it means and you'll get a variety of responses: some think it refers to lamb's lettuce, but they're wrong.* Amsterdams Vet *is actually a name for turnips harvested early. These are the tender plants that are thinned out from the rows of turnip shoots to give the rest of them room to grow.*

Ingredients

- 100 g lamb's lettuce or young spinach
- 100 g Amsterdams Vet (turnip greens)
- 2 sticks celery
- 1 bunch little radishes
- 1 pickled apple
- 2 tsp lime or lemon juice
- 100-150 g crumbled blue cheese

For the sauce:

- 3 tbsp mayonnaise
- 3 tbsp crème fraîche
- salt
- freshly-ground white pepper

Rinse the lamb's lettuce or spinach and the Amsterdams Vet in plenty of cold water. Remove all the stalks and stems. Dry the leaves as thoroughly as possible, ideally in a salad spinner, and place them in a mixing bowl.

Make a julienne (short thin strips) of the celery, radishes and apple. Douse the apple sticks in lime or lemon juice.

Stir the celery, radish and apple in a mixing bowl in a wide, open motion. Scatter the cheese over the mix.

Make the sauce, by mixing mayonnaise with lightly-beaten crème fraîche. Add a little salt and pepper.

Serve the vegetables separately from the sauce.

LENTILS WITH AMSTERDAM ONIONS AND SAUSAGE

Linzen met Amsterdamse uien en worst

[ˈlɪnzən mɛt ˈæmstədæmsə ˈœyən ɛn wɔrst]

Serves 4

Any Dutchman will tell you that Amsterdam onions are yellow. They get their hue from the addition of saffron, a spice that arrived in Northern Europe early from Arab cuisine. Pickled onions are white. Pickling was a necessary technique in the past to conserve vegetables and other foodstuffs.

Ingredients
250 g lentils
3 bay leaves
1 l tap water
300 g small grilling sausages (braadworst)
250 g cherry tomatoes, still on the vine
340 g Amsterdam onions (from jar)
1 tbsp fine mustard

Place the lentils, bay leaves and water in a pan. Bring to the boil and cook the lentils until they are al dente, approx. 20 minutes. Strain through a sieve and remove the bay leaves. Place the lentils in a bowl and baste them with mustard.
Take the skins off of the sausages and dice the sausage meat. Halve the tomatoes. Fry the sausage meat in a non-stick frying pan with no oil or butter, for 8 minutes, until golden brown and tender. For the final 3 minutes, add the tomatoes.
Drain the onions, halve them and add to the lentils.
Finally, add the sausage mixture from the pan.

tip This dish can be enjoyed hot, lukewarm or cold.

MARROWFAT PEAS WITH ONION AND APPLE

Amsterdams Zoete met uien en appel

[æmstəˈdæms ˈzutə mɛt ‘œyən ɛn ˈɑpəl]

Serves 4 as a side dish

Amsterdams Zoete *is a fantastic old variety of marrowfat pea, named to reflect that it was traded at Amsterdam market in the old days. Therefore, this variety must have been first created somewhere near the market. As the Dutch name suggests, this is a sweet-tasting pea. For the amateur market gardeners among us, the seed is available commercially and you can try your hand at growing the variety yourself.*
If you don't have Amsterdams Zoete *available, you can of course use any regular marrowfat peas instead.*

Ingredients

1 leek
3 tomatoes
1 tbsp cooking oil
2 tsp curry powder
1 large jar marrowfat peas
1 apple
10 Amsterdam onions

Clean the leek and cut it into rings.
Rinse and dice the tomatoes.
Heat the oil in a skillet and sweat the leeks in it, not too hard.
Add the curry powder and briefly braise the diced tomato in the mix.
Drain the peas.
Peel and dice the apple.
Halve the Amsterdam onions.
Mix the apple, onions and peas through the leek-and-tomato mix and heat through.

AMSTERDAM KALE STEW WITH ONIONS, BEANS AND BOCK BEER

Amsterdamse stoofschotel boerenkool met uien

[æmstədæms'ə 'stofsxotəl 'burən'kol mɛt 'œyən]

Serves 4

This kale-based Amsterdam stew dates from the era when the city was mainly peopled by hardscrabble labourers, journeymen and dockers. What they needed was good solid food. They certainly got their nourishment from this stew, particularly in its original version, which was less luxurious than the one we present to you here.

Ingredients

400 g mince (half pork, half beef)
meatball spice mix (gehakt-kruiden) or salt and freshly-ground pepper
100 g bacon rinds (spekreepjes)
2 tbsp tomato puree
½ tbsp curry powder
400 g Amsterdam onions
400 g young marrowfat peas
300 g sliced kale
200 g sliced runner beans
400 g baked beans (sold in the Netherlands as 'witte bonen in tomatensaus')
30 cl Bock beer
100 g mature cheese, grated

Form mini-meatballs from the mince and season with the spice mix or salt and pepper. Warm a skillet, with no oil or butter in it, and fry the bacon rinds in it for approx. 3 minutes until crispy. Add the mini-meatballs and fry them for approx. 5 minutes until brown all over.

Add in the tomato puree and curry powder and keep frying for about one more minute. Drain the Amsterdam onions.

Rinse and drain the peas. Add the kale, runner beans, onions, peas, baked beans and Bock beer and bring it all to the boil.

Let it all simmer on a low flame with the lid on for 10 minutes.

After serving onto plates, scatter the grated cheese on top.

JEWISH *LATKES*

Joodse latkes • [ˈjotsə ˈlɑtkəs]

Serves 4 as a snack

Hanukkah is a Jewish festival, lasting for eight-days, which commemorates the rededication of the Jerusalem Temple in 164 BC. At that time, the Jews were being severely oppressed by Hellenistic kings, who defiled and ravaged the Second Temple. Under the leadership of Judas Maccabaeus, the Temple was retaken. During Hanukkah, a nine-branched candlestick, the hanukkiah, has its candles lit one per day. For this reason, Hanukkah is also known as the Festival of Lights. One of the delicacies enjoyed at Hanukkah is latkes, potato pancakes.

Ingredients

- 8 medium-sized, firm-cooking potatoes
- 1 large onion
- 1 egg
- 3 tbsp flour
- salt and freshly-ground black pepper
- 2 tbsp olive oil

Peel the potatoes and coarsely grate them.
Do the same with the onion and add it to the potatoes.
Wrap the mixture in a clean tea towel and wring as much moisture as possible out of it.
Add to this a beaten egg and the flour.
Season to taste with salt and pepper, and form into little flat pancakes.
Fry them until crispy in a neutral oil with a high smoke point. If necessary, press them down a little while frying. Let them drain a moment by setting them on kitchen paper. Serve warm.

tip Scrumptious with smoked salmon and sour cream.

JEWISH PICKLE SELLERS

In the lead-up to the Second World War, and afterwards too, street vendors called door to door every day selling their wares. The familiar faces on the rounds were the baker, the grocer, the bread roll (*Berlinerbol*) man, the milkman, the knife grinder and in summer the ice cream man. One member of this small army of wandering tradesmen was the *zuurjood*, the Jewish pickle seller. One wouldn't call someone a 'pickle Jew' nowadays, but no harm was meant by it back then. The pickle seller offered herring, gherkins, onions, cucumbers and liver sausage; all pickled, of course. The well-known Amsterdam onions (*Amsterdamse uien*), still popular today, date from this era. Pickles were a characteristically Jewish trade. It began in Poland, Lithuania, Ukraine and Russia, where Jews had the custom of preserving fresh vegetables in acidic liquid. This conserved the vegetables, allowing them to be kept and sold for longer. Eastern European Jews who came here as refugees imported this food preparation technique to Amsterdam. The pickle trade thus became a real Amsterdam tradition.

Callers at the door were not only salesmen; some came to take unwanted stuff away, including the peelings man and the rag-and-bone man (often known as a *voddenjood*). The peelings man or *schillenboer* came down the street with a cart to collect vegetable waste to go into pigswill. The rag-and-bone man called out for old bits of cloth, for paper or cleaning cloth manufacture.

De zuurventer

(The Pickle Seller), by Johan Coenraad Braakensiek (1858-1940) ▸

Sausage and pickle

AMSTERDAM ONIONS

Amsterdamse uitjes

[æmstəˈdæmsə ˈœycəs]

To make a jar of approx. ¾ litres

Amsterdam onions are delicious. They're great on their own, as a finger food, with a herring (which is at its best eaten by the stall where you buy it), with cheese, on beef sausage or on a hamburger. They're also lovely in a regular salad, a potato salad or a beef stew. They're not hard to make at home, either.

Ingredients

250 g shallots
25 cl white wine vinegar
25 cl apple cider vinegar
6 threads of saffron
1 bay leaf
1 tbsp mustard seed
2 tbsp sugar
pinch of salt

Place the shallots in a mixing bowl and pour boiling water over them. Leave them to soak for 1 minute and then strain. Now remove the skins and transfer them to a jar.
Pour both kinds of vinegar into a pan and add the herbs, sugar and salt. Bring the mixture to the boil.
As soon as it starts to boil, remove the pan from the heat and immediately pour its contents over the onions in the jar.
Let the jar cool off before sealing it tight.
Keep the jar in the fridge. The onions will be edible after three weeks. They will remain good for six months in the fridge.

◂ ***Previous page:*** *Herring and pickle cart*

PICKLED LIVER SAUSAGE

Leverworst in het zuur

[ˈlevərˈwɔrst in hɛt zyr]

To make a jar of approx. one litre

There are plenty of foodstuffs you can pickle. Pickles tend to be sweet and sour, because sugar (or sweetener) is usually added to the vinegar. All kinds of fruit and vegetables can be pickled, including tomatoes, bell peppers, onions, chilli peppers, red cabbage, cucumbers, courgettes, lemons and dried fruit such as raisins. But even liver sausage can be pickled; a real Amsterdam Jewish tradition. This recipe is another of the easy ones to replicate at home.

Ingredients

400 cl spice vinegar
20 cl water
sugar (if desired)
2 bay leaves
6 black peppercorns
2 cloves
1 onion, cut into half rings
1 to 2 cloves garlic, sliced
1 sliceable liver sausage (*leverworst*) of 500 g

Pour the vinegar and water into a pan and add the sugar, bay leaves, peppercorns, cloves, onion and garlic.
Bring to the boil and gently simmer the mixture for 5 minutes.
Cut the liver sausage into slices and place them in a thoroughly cleaned jar.
Let the herb and vinegar mix cool and pour it over the sausage.
Be careful that the sausage slices remain intact.
Seal the jar tightly and place it in the fridge for 3 to 5 days.

tip You can use ready-made pickling herbs (*inmaakkruiden*) in place of the spice mix. If you do, then the quantity to use is one sachet or one tablespoonful.

MAKING BEEF SAUSAGE

Ossenworst • [ˈɔssənˈwɔrst]

Makes 1

There's something contradictory about beef sausage. Most people would describe this raw sausage as a real Jewish speciality, since it's possible to make a kosher variant of it. Originally (that's in the seventeenth century), it was really made from ox meat, hence the name ossenworst. *Technically, an ox is a bull that's been castrated to make it a less jumpy plough animal. There's a catch, though. One of the 613 mitsvot (commandments) of the Torah is that a male animal must not be castrated. There appears to be doubt about the kosher status of the sausage, then. Besides, to be kosher, meat has to be taken from the front of a bull, because the hindquarters are regarded as unclean. Whether kosher or not,* ossenworst *has come to be seen as an Amsterdam Jewish classic. In the seventeenth century, oxen were imported from Denmark and Germany, and the sausage was prepared with spices from the Dutch East Indies.*

Ingredients

1 g sugar
2.5 g pepper
2.5 g mace*
10 g nitrate salt (sold in the Netherlands as *kleurzout*)
500 g beef loin

* You could replace the 2.5 g of mace with a mixture of 1 g mace, 1 g clove and 1 g nutmeg

Grind the sugar, spices and salt very fine. It's best to use a coffee grinder, but a mortar and pestle will also do. Cut up the meat until it has the texture of coarse mince. Ideally, use a meat grinder. Loosely blend the sugar-spice-salt mix through the mince, ensuring that the meat's texture does not suffer.
Place the mince on a piece of cling film and tightly roll it into a proper sausage shape. Pinch the ends closed.
Let the sausage ferment for 24 hours at approx. 20 ° C.
After this ripening, refrigerate it.

N.B.: Consume this beef sausage within two days!

AMSTERDAM CARPACCIO

Amsterdamse carpaccio

[æmstəˈdæmsə karˈpaco]

Serves 2

This starter, inspired by the old-fashioned Dutch wooden snack boards, is a real Mokum dish, as it combines beef sausage with Amsterdam onions.

Ingredients

12 slices beef sausage
2 handfuls grated mature cheese
8 Amsterdam onions
2 tbsp mayonnaise
1 tbsp mustard
2 tbsp fresh parsley, minced

Place 6 slices of beef sausage on a sheet of aluminium foil. Place another sheet of foil on top of that and, with a rolling pin, roll them out to form a nice round sheet.
Make another beef carpaccio the same way and then place the both of them on one plate each.
Dice the Amsterdam onions.
Mix the mayonnaise with the mustard.
Take a tablespoonful of mayonnaise, divide it evenly across each plate and distribute the diced onions on top.
Sprinkle the plates with cheese.
Finally, garnish the top with the minced parsley.

HERRING SALAD WITH SHRIMP

Haringsalade met garnalen

[ˈharɪŋsaˈladə mɛt xɑrˈnalən]

Serves 4 as a side dish

Once the technique of sousing herrings had been invented, the fish could be gutted, salted and packed into barrels at sea. Once the catch was landed, herring packers opened the barrels and checked over the contents. If necessary, some of the catch was soused again or discarded. The herring packers were strictly checked by inspectors, and sported a medal indicating their competence to carry out their work. To this day, herring packers are a recognised specialism in the Dutch economy, with their own collective bargaining agreement.

Ingredients

2 potatoes
2 tomatoes
½ green bell pepper
2 tbsp mayonnaise
2 tbsp yoghurt
salt and pepper
1 tbsp minced chive
3 gutted herrings
100 g smallest Dutch shrimps
1 head of curly leaf lettuce

Boil the potatoes for approx. 20 minutes until tender, cool them off and dice them.
Rub the tomatoes with the spices, plunge them in boiling water for 10 seconds and then remove their skins. Dice the tomatoes after removing the pips.
Rinse the bell pepper, remove the ribs and dice the flesh.
Mix the mayonnaise and yoghurt into a sauce and season them to taste with salt and pepper.
Then stir the chives, tomato, potato and pepper through it.
Refrigerate this mixture for at least half an hour.
Just before serving, dice the herring and stir both the herring and the shrimps through the potato mixture.

De haringpakkerstoren (Herring packers Tower) ▸

THE JEWISH QUARTER

We keep bumping into Jewish influences on Amsterdam cuisine and food in this book. While the Jews were not persecuted here, the circumstances in which most of them had to live were miserable. Until the twentieth century, they lived in what could easily be called a slum: the area between the Central Station, Kloveniersburgwal, Waterlooplein, Valkenburgerstraat and Prins Hendrikkade. In the vernacular, this part of the city was the *Jodenhoek*, 'Jewish Corner'. (Accordingly, the local argot spoken here was known as *Jodenhoeks*.) Its inhabitants lived in crushing poverty.

Besides, although the Jews were fairly safe here, there were plenty of restrictions on them. Initially, they were not allowed to worship openly, and had to open synagogues that were not recognisable as such. They were not admitted into guilds either, which obliged them to practise trades that were not unionised. This is what drove many of them to become merchants.

'Merchant' makes one think of a man of standing, but bear in mind that these were mostly street hawkers, pedlars or rag-and-bone men (*voddenjoden*). Jews were also able to make loans, grind diamonds, butcher meat and trade fruit and vegetables.

Among many Amsterdammers, there is the custom of not cooking on Saturdays and instead making luxury sandwiches with plenty of different fillings. This might well be a vestige of the city's Jewish heritage. Sabbath, the weekly day of rest, begins before sundown on Friday and from then on, one may not work. Cooking is work, too. This means that the food for Saturday has to be already prepared by then. So, the habit of eating sandwiches or chips on Saturday probably has Jewish origins.

Jodenhoek (Jewish quarter) bustling with street vendors ▸

Sweet treats

AMSTERDAMER PITMOPPEN AND FRAU ANTJE

Amsterdamse pitmoppen

[ˈæmstəˈdæmsə ˈpɪtˈmɔppən]

To make approx. 25 *pitmoppen*

Anyone in Germany who wants to make Amsterdamer Pitmoppen *(almond biscuits) can easily find the recipe in one of the many* Frau Antje Kochbücher, *'Antje's Cookbooks'. (*Frau Antje *is an advertising character in Germany to personify Dutch cooking. She is a representation of a farmer's wife wearing the old Dutch costume.) The Germans also know them as* Mandelplätzchen nach Amsterdamer Art. *Here's the recipe for* Amsterdamse pitmoppen.

Ingredients

150 g butter
150 g sugar
1 egg
lemon, and grated rind of a quarter lemon
pinch of salt
250 g flour
1 knife-tip of baking powder
1 egg, yolk only
100 g almonds, peeled

Cream the butter and blend the sugar through it.
Add the egg yolk, grated lemon rind, salt and the flour that has been sieved together with the baking powder, and stir them all through the mix. Knead the dough into a stiff 'sandcake' dough. Make it into a ball, wrap it in aluminium foil and let it rest for about two hours. Preheat the oven to 200 °C.
Place a sheet of baking paper on the baking tray.
Roll the dough into sheets of about half a centimetre (a quarter of an inch) thickness. Cut squares of 3 x 3 cm out of these, or cut the dough out using cookie cutters.
Loosen out an egg yolk with a fork and baste the cookies with it. Place two half almonds on each cookie.
Place the cookies on the tray and bake them until golden brown, approx. 10 to 15 minutes.

SPICY JORDAAN CAKE

Jordanese kruidkoek • [jɔrdanˈesə ˈkrœytkuk]

Makes 1

Sometimes, an investigative reporter proves that a good story is just made up. This is what happened with Aunt Daatje's recipe for spicy Jordaan cake, the pride and joy of her family. As far as her relatives knew, she made it from her own secret recipe. However, after Daatje's death, it came to light that the recipe was simply taken from Miss Wannée's Amsterdamsche Huishoudschool cookbook *described earlier in this book.*

Ingredients

150 g blue and/or golden raisins
100 g currants
125 g butter, room temperature
2 large eggs
125 g dark brown caster sugar
1 tbsp ground cloves (*gruis*, 'grit')
1 tbsp finely-grated nutmeg
1 tbsp powdered ginger root
1 tbsp powdered cinnamon
125 g flour, strained
1 knife-tip of salt
2 tbsp gossamer-fine candied orange peel snippets (*oranje snippers*)
cake form of 24 cm (12") diameter

Rinse the raisins and currants a few times in plenty of cold water. Drain them in a sieve and dry them out as well as possible. Preheat the oven to 180 °C.

In a mixing bowl, stir the butter into a light, creamy mass. Beat the eggs, one by one, into the butter using a small whisk. Keep beating for a further 4 to 5 minutes after adding the last egg. Sieve the caster sugar and spice mix above the butter mix and fold it in with a spatula. Gradually add the sieved flour, orange snippets, raisins and currants. Butter the cake form and fill it with the dough. With the convex side of a spoon, smooth the surface. Place the cake form on the middle tray of the preheated oven. Bake the cake for approx. 60 to 65 minutes until golden brown and done. Remove from the oven and leave the cake to stand for another 10 minutes. Remove from form; cool it on a cake grid.

AMSTERDAM KOGGETJES

Amsterdamse koggetjes • [ɑmstər'dɑmsə 'kɔxəcəs]

Makes 75-80

The Amsterdamse koggetjes, *also known as 'nougatine', was quite an invention. In 1934, a contest was announced to come up with a new kind of cake that would typify Amsterdam. The koggetje (named after Amsterdam's city crest, which portrays a* kogge *or cog, the definitive cargo ship of the Late Middle Ages;* *see p. 17**) was proclaimed the winning entry. This prompted a huge row between the Catholic Bakers' Union and the secular bakers' union. Members of the latter had designed a special tin for the new cake, and the Catholics were banned from selling it. So the Catholic bakers came up with their own cake instead, shaped like an Amsterdam house gable. And it had its own tin, naturally.*

Ingredients

- 280 g Zeeland flour (*Zeeuwse bloem*), or low protein wheat flour
- 250 g caster sugar
- 230 g butter, room temperature
- 4 g vanilla
- 2 g salt
- 1 medium-sized egg
- 80 g nougat*, in finely-chopped pieces

* caramelised, hardened sugar syrup

Make sure all ingredients are at room temperature before you start. Preheat the oven to 170 °C.
Sift the flour and tap the lumps out of the sugar.
In a mixing bowl, turn the butter over with a spatula until it is a creamy mass. Add vanilla, salt and sugar and mix the mass into a homogenous whole (you might like to warm it in a bain-marie). Through this, mix first the egg, then the flour, and finally the finely-chopped nougat.
Fill an icing bag with the mix and squeeze out dollops of approx. 10 g each on a baking tray with a sheet of baking paper on it. Bake these biscuits for 10 to 15 minutes until the edges begin to darken. After baking, briefly cool them and then quickly remove them from the baking tray.

JEWISH BUTTER CAKE

Joodse boterkoek • ['jotsə 'botərkuk]

Serves approx. 12

Boterkoek *is a particularly Dutch speciality; there's no equivalent of it in the neighbouring countries. Evidently, it was a treat for the lower orders:* boterkoek *was not sold by upmarket bakeries or suave tearooms in the old days. Authorities tell us that self-respecting cookery shops didn't even sell the ubiquitous round* boterkoek *tray in the old days; it seems they thought it beneath them. Claudia Roden, an expert on Jewish cuisine, included* boterkoek *as the only Dutch recipe in her book* De Joodse keuken. *After all, it is Jewish: this was a sweet served on the Sabbath. Although it did have added ginger on Jewish tables!*

Ingredients

250 g butter at room temperature
150 g white caster sugar
150 g self-raising cake flour
150 g regular flour
pinch of salt
100 g candied ginger, in pieces
1 egg, beaten

Preheat the oven to 200 °C.
Dice the butter and place it in a batter bowl.
Mix the remaining ingredients together with dough hooks to form a consistent dough.
Grease a *boterkoek* tray with butter.
Fill the form and push the dough well into it with the convex side of a damp spoon.
Glaze the top with beaten egg.
Bake the *boterkoek* for approx. 25 minutes until golden brown and tasty.

tip Before placing the *boterkoek* in the oven, you might like to score points on it with a sharp knife or put lines on it with a fork.

GINGER *BOLUS*

Gemberbolussen • [ˈxɛmbərˈbolʏsən]

Makes 12

The Dutch name for this sweet bakery product, bolus, *is probably a borrowing from Yiddish* bole, *meaning 'fine baking'. In other parts of the Netherlands, the bolus was already being sold by Sephardic bakers in the early seventeenth century; it arrived in Amsterdam later. The general Dutch version of a bolus was, and still is, made from bread dough with added sugar syrup and cinnamon; the Amsterdam Jewish* bolus *has a ginger filling. We've already seen how prominent ginger is in Jewish cuisine, such as in* boterkoek. *However, ginger biscuits (*gemberkoekjes*) are also of Jewish origin. In fact there's another version of the* bolus, *filled with orangeade (sweetened almond paste with orange). Connoisseurs insist on serving a bolus warm.*

Ingredients

10 cl milk
5 g dried yeast
4 g sugar (1 tsp)
250 g patent flour and some more for dusting
1 medium-sized egg, beaten
50 g butter at room temperature
6 g salt
400 g stem ginger
150 g almonds
50 g butter, melted
5 cl ginger syrup
3 tbsp white caster sugar

Extra equipment:
Muffin tin or pan with 12 depressions

Warm the milk with yeast and sugar until lukewarm (no hotter than 40 °C). Briefly stir it up and leave to stand for 10 minutes until the surface begins lightly frothing.
Sieve the flour over a batter bowl and add milk, egg and butter. Mix the whole lot into a dense dough.
Add salt and knead the dough by hand for 10 minutes until it is stretchy (or for 5 minutes in a worktop, not handheld, mixer with dough hooks). Optionally add a little flour if the dough is excessively sticky.

Place the dough in a mixing bowl, sprinkle with a little flour and loosely cover with cling film. Let the dough rise for one hour at room temperature.
Thoroughly drain the ginger root (reserving the syrup) and puree it in a blender, together with the almonds, to form a thick paste. Divide the melted butter and ginger syrup across the muffin forms. Divide the dough into twelve equal balls. Roll them in the caster sugar and, using your fingertips, flatten them into oval discs of about 12 cm (6") diameter. Along the long edge, fill the sheets of dough with a generous dollop of the ginger paste. Roll the dough around the paste like a cigar and coil it into the muffin forms like a cigar (or tie it in a knot).
Leave the dough to rise in the forms for a further 30 minutes. Preheat the oven to 200 °C. Place a small bowl of boiling water at the bottom of the oven (for the steam). Bake the *bolussen* for 20 minutes in the middle of the oven until golden brown. Cool in the form.

BUCKWHEAT CRÊPES

Boekende flensjes • ['bukɛndə 'flɛnʃəs]

Makes approx. 4

The Golden Age playwright Gerbrand Bredero wrote Moortje *in 1615, a drama set in Amsterdam. It incudes a portrayal of a* Sinterklaas *evening where a character says: 'Our boy had so many treats to eat, he couldn't believe his luck: figs, nuts, buckwheat* flensjes *and other such delicacies.'*
Buckwheat flensjes, *known by a variety of names such as* boekweit-flensjes, boekende flensjes *and* bokkende flensjes, *were an Amsterdam speciality baked on* Sinterklaas *evening and at New Year. They were a real treat, as long as they were fried with bits of apple and currant in them and not cabbage.*

Ingredients

100 g buckwheat flour
pinch of sea salt
2 eggs
30 cl water
1 apple, grated
handful of currants or raisins
oil or butter for the frying

Place the flour and salt in a mixing bowl and first mix in the eggs, then the water.
Keep on stirring until you have a smooth batter. Add a little extra water if desired.
Add the apple and currants or raisins.
Let the batter rest for 10 minutes or so before starting to fry, to make it less brittle.
Heat the butter or oil in a frying pan and fry up the *flensjes* one by one.

Detail of painting by Jan Steen, c. 1666. Festival of St Nicholas (Sinterklaas). The girl in the foreground has been rewarded with a doll; the lads on the left get a beating for a naughty year. ▸

AMSTERDAM GINGERBREAD

Amsterdamse korstjes • [amstər'damsə 'kɔrscəs]

Makes approx. 15

On their birthdays, orphan girls at the Burgerweeshuis *(Municipal Orphanage), whose site is now occupied by the Amsterdam Museum, were given an* Amsterdams korstje. *Actually, the only orphans admitted here had been born to well-heeled Amsterdammers; there were no places for foundlings or the orphans of the poor.*

Amsterdamse korstjes *are a halfway house between* taaitaai *and* ontbijtkoek, *two other gingerbread specialities. An old kitchen notebook has preserved a lovely recipe for it. It calls for a combination of cookie dough and slegt, an old word for leftover bits of old biscuit. There was no baking soda in those days, so alum was used.*

Ingredients

325 g honey
60 g brown caster sugar
450 g rye flour
4 g baking soda or 12 g baking powder
20 g koekkruiden (ginger mix for biscuits)
80 g water
pinch of salt
1 egg, beaten

Preheat the oven to 200 °C.
Mix up the honey, sugar and water and bring to the boil. Let it simmer for a moment.
Then mix the flour, soda, ginger mix for biscuits and salt through it to form a homogenous mass.
Roll out the dough on a baking tray with a sheet of baking paper on it, forming a flat layer.
Glaze the layer with the beaten egg and bake it for 15 to 20 minutes.
Then remove from the oven and cut into bars.

The kitchen at the Burgerweeshuis (Municipal Orphanage) ▸

BEER, WINE AND JENEVER

Even back in the Middle Ages, the water supply was often so filthy in the major cities that it was unfit for human consumption. This is how beer became the main drink. In fact, it wasn't just something to sip: it has been calculated that around 300 litres of it were drunk per person per year. Nowadays, that figure is just 83 litres. However, the alcohol content was much lower then, comparable with what we'd call 'special events beer' nowadays, at around 2%. Beer was mainly brewed at home in the old days, by housewives, but commercial breweries did arise in mediaeval Amsterdam.

Wine was reserved for the upper classes. Until the sixteenth century, wine consumption in the Netherlands has been estimated at 20 litres per capita per year. The assumption is that in the Golden Age, when Amsterdam and its inhabitants became wealthier by the year, wine consumption shot up.

In fact, seventeenth-century Amsterdam had a high density of taverns. These *tapperijen* number 400 to 500 in historical sources, which works out at one *tapperij* for every 200 to 250 inhabitants!

As is often the case with tipples, jenever was celebrated for its medicinal qualities, no matter what the ailment. In *De lof der jenever* (In Praise of Jenever), by Robert Hennebo (1718), we read the line *Jenever in de morgenstond: verfrist en maakt den mensch gezond* ('There's nothing like a morning gin to keep you well and strong of limb'). In the eighteenth century, jenever consumption got out of hand, eventually coming to be seen as a menace to public health. This was among the poorest, of course, because as with Hogarth's 'Gin Lane' in London, jenever was for the needy folk.

After Johan Braakensiek's 'Ach vader lief, toe drink niet meer'
('O father dear, lay off the drink') ▸

VERGUNNING
VRIJ
OUDE GENEVER

Spirits

PIKKETANUSSIE

[pɪkə'tanʏzi]

Borrel, neut, klare, oorlam, pikketanussie, hartversterkertje, jajem, hassebassie: these are just some of the Dutch nicknames for a glass of jenever. With there being so many names for it, you can safely conclude that jenever has been a well-loved drink here for centuries. Amsterdam was a major centre of jenever distilling, an industry that was flourishing as far back as the seventeenth-century Golden Age.

Jenever is served in a diminutive glass: a tulip-shaped *kelkje* ('wee goblet') or a small tumbler. Traditionally, one is supposed to fill the glass to the brim, giving the drink a real 'head'. This brim-full glass is fondly called 'a peek over the River IJ'. This is the origin of the landlords' custom of placing the empty glass on the bar first and then filling it. The customer leans forward and, without touching the glass with his hands, slurps the 'head' off.

Jenever and beer go together well, but go easy on it! For a very good reason this combination is known as a *kopstoot*, 'bang on the head'. To serve it, the landlord places a jenever glass alongside your beer and you sip them alternately. A jenever tradition with even more wow is the *duikboot*, 'submarine'. There are three ways to serve this. The simplest is just to empty your jenever into your beer. You can also carefully trickle a glass of jenever into your beer until it settles on the bottom. Most spectacular, though, is this version: fill a jenever glass to the brim and place an inverted beer glass on top of it. Make sure the rim of the jenever glass is in contact with the bottom of the beer glass. Then, in a fluid but determined movement, invert the whole lot and start filling the beer glass. At some point, your jenever glass will upend itself and you'll get a shot in your beer.

◂ ***Previous page:*** *Two pikketanussies and two beers*

Gezondheid!
LUCAS BOLS
Z.O. GENEVER
BOLS
BOLS
ELKEN DAG EEN GLAASJE

AMSTERDAM LIQUEURS

Makes approx. 1 litre

Amsterdam had more than a just flourishing jenever industry: in the seventeenth and eighteenth centuries, liqueur distillation was also big here. In 1879, there were a grand total of thirty distilleries in operation, making Amsterdam the hub of the trade. As well as serving the local and national market, these distilleries exported abroad. The big names were (and still are) 't Lootsje (founded by Erven Lucas Bols), De Drie Fleschjes (H. Bootz), Van Wees, and Wijnand Fockink.
It stood to reason that Amsterdam should be such a big player in this market, given its status as one of the world's leading ports. All the ingredients needed for distilling were on hand: exotic fruit, spices, and of course a large population of the elite who constitute the main clientele for the finished product.

Ingredients

500 cl rum, vodka or brandy
flavour enhancers (fruit, nuts, spices, cocoa beans, coffee beans, or whatever you fancy)
25 cl sugar syrup (from a supermarket or off-licence)

Half-fill with your spirit of choice a carefully-cleaned, sealable bottle, or wide-rimmed jar with hinged, sealable lid.
Dice the fruit very finely. Roughly chop the nuts. Cut the citrus zest into small bits.
Add the seasonings and seal the jar or bottle.
The proportion of ingredients should be roughly as follows: two parts spirit, two to four parts seasoning and one part sugar syrup.
Put the jar away for a couple of weeks, but invert it daily.
Then strain the fruit out
and finally add the syrup.
Transfer the liqueur to an attractive carafe or bottle in front of your guests and serve.

HOT BEERENBURG COCKTAIL

Beerenburg haardvuurtje

['berənbʏrx 'hartvyrcə]

Serves approx. 5-6

A drink to keep the doctor away on bone-chilling days!

Beerenburg, which is widely assumed to be as Frisian as can be, was actually invented in Amsterdam. Hendrik Beerenburg ran an herbs and spices warehouse on Stroomarkt in the city from 1645 onwards. He sold herb mixes of his own creation, one of which gained quite some popularity: his Opregte Maag-Kruiden, *or 'Salutary Herbs for the Stomach'. Those who bought it swore by it as a cure-all. The herbs were infused in jenever, and the result came to be known by Hendrik's own surname: Beerenburg. One can imagine less pleasant medicines! Jenever brewers and apothecaries alike started imitating this concoction. It spawned a range of other herbal mixes, although they were not allowed to use the spelling Beerenburg and so got away with the variants Beerenburger or Berenburg.*
It was in Friesland that this drink achieved its greatest popularity.

Ingredients

1 orange
4 cloves
1 cinnamon stick
3 star anise
30 cl Beerenburg
80 cl cloudy apple juice

Scrub the orange clean and cut it into slices.
Place the orange, spices, Beerenburg and apple juice in a pan and let it steep for 30 minutes on a low flame, without letting it come to simmer.
Divide the drink, including the orange slices, into glasses (which must be heat-resistant) or cups, and serve.

AMSTERDAM TOASTED SANDWICH WITH A GLASS OF BEER

Amsterdamse tosti met een glas bier

[amstər'damsə ˈtɔsti mɛt ən xlas bir]

Makes 4

Amsterdam has played host to no end of breweries over the years. In the Middle Ages, the city was a major transhipment port for beer, in addition to grain and wood. Count Willem II of Holland imposed the law in 1323 that ships importing beer destined for the Low Countries must call at Amsterdam. This turned the city into the Low Counries' beer importing hub. However, the imports came under pressure from tariffs and wars, which will certainly have provided a stimulus to local beer brewing. In 1685, there were no fewer than 23 breweries in Amsterdam. Even after that, many new breweries continued to be opened there, including famous ones. Some carried on for a couple of centuries, but in the end they were snapped up by Heineken one by one.
The toasted sandwich below can of course be served with any drink you like, but we'd recommend your favourite beer.

Ingredients
2 tbsp mustard
2 tbsp mayonnaise
8 slices bread
100 g mature cheese, sliced
200 g beef sausage
8 Amsterdam onions, drained, and diced or sliced

Blend the mustard with the mayonnaise and spread it on the sandwiches.
Cover half of each sandwich with cheese, sausage and onions, and finish off with the other four slices.
Toast the sandwiches golden brown and slice them diagonally.

AMSTERDAM COCKTAIL

[amstər'dam 'kɔktel]

Serves 5-6

Korenwijn *is, despite its name, not corn wine but a variety of jenever. Traditionally, it is often drunk as an accompaniment to herring. The salty taste of this oily fish really comes into its own after a stout swallow of this spirit. However, you are of course free to take more than one glug.* Korenwijn *has a lot more character to it than regular jenever, as it has more herbs in the mash. Sometimes,* korenwijn *is matured in wooden casks, and then its smoothness approaches that of malt whisky. A key (and obligatory) ingredient of it is malt wine: the law requires* korenwijn *to be at least 51% malt wine. We can be reasonably sure that today's* korenwijn *bears a close resemblance to the taste of the jenevers that were distilled in centuries gone by.*
Here's a recipe for a genuine Amsterdam cocktail.

Ingredients

5 cl Bols Corenwyn six-year reserve
2.5 cl Cointreau
2.5 cl fresh orange juice
a dash of Angostura bitters
orange peel

Extra equipment:
cocktail shaker
Martini glasses

Fill a shaker with ice cubes.
Add the Corenwyn, Cointreau, orange juice and a dash of Angostura Bitters and shake until the shaker is properly cold to the touch.
Strain through a sieve into a Martini glass and garnish with a thin slice of orange peel.

AMSTERDAM RIOTS

The Potato Riots

The unrest that broke out in Amsterdam in 1917 later came to be known as the Potato Riots. A poor harvest, reduced potato supply lines due to the First World War in neighbouring countries, and the growth in exports combined to make the potato, the unrivalled staple of the Dutch masses, scarce. On 28 June, working-class neighbourhoods sought a way to vent their frustration and despair. A group, largely composed of women, hit the streets and pillaged a potato barge.

Over the next few days, the unrest and demonstrations spread across the whole city. On 2 July, an enraged mob from the Dam rampaged its way to the vegetable market in Marnixstraat, only to encounter a large contingent of policemen on the beat. Fighting ensued, stones flew through the air and shop windows were smashed. The police aimed their pistols to hit, not as warning shots, and the atmosphere became worse and worse as the day wore into evening. Finally, fresh supplies calmed the frayed nerves. The outcome was ten deaths and 114 casualties.

The Eel Riots

31 years previously, again in July, the Eel Riots broke out in the Jordaan neighbourhood. However, this had nothing to do with scarcity; it was a response to a ban on the sport of *palingtrekken*, 'eel-pulling'.

The rules of this plebeian game were simple: a live eel was tied to a cable suspended above a canal, and people went out in boats to try to liberate the slippery creature. The denizens of Jordaan cared little for the outlawing of this 'game' and carried on regardless. When the police showed up to break up the match, disorder ensued. Even soldiers were dispatched to the scene. The riots went on for two full days and were so serious that the death toll mounted to 24. The deeper cause of these riots was the atrocious living conditions in the slums of Jordaan.

Amsterdam Police attending to civil unrest during the 1917 Potato Riots.

BINNEN BANTAMMERSTRAAT: AMSTERDAM'S CHINATOWN

The first Chinese started arriving in the Netherlands in the early 1900s. They were mostly stokers on steamships. They were hardworking, earned little and concerned themselves with nobody except each other. They spoke a little English and no Dutch at all. On shore, in Rotterdam or Amsterdam, they stayed at boarding houses. Their Amsterdam addresses were in and around Binnen Bantammerstraat.

In the 1930s, due to the Depression and the transition from steam to diesel-powered ships, many Chinese seamen found themselves unemployed. Some went out on the streets selling peanuts they had roasted themselves. They became known as *Pinda-Chinezen*, "Peanut Chinese".

A Chinese restaurant catering to non-Chinese had already been opened on Binnen Bantammerstraat before this time; its owner had given up his boarding house to run this business.

After WWII, most of the Chinese in the Netherlands (which included Hong Kong and Overseas Chinese) were involved in the restaurant trade. Binnen Bantammerstraat retained its status as Amsterdam's Chinatown. The residents themselves dubbed it Tong Yan Kai, 'Chinese Street'. In addition to its many restaurants, it played host to illegal gambling dens and opium dens. These dens opened their doors only to Chinese.

Chinese eateries began popping up elsewhere in the city, and they got an enormous boost when East Indies families, both Dutch and mixed-heritage, started returning here in the 1950s after Indonesia gained its independence. The Chinese restaurateurs in the Netherlands, who had previously offered Mainland Chinese fare, responded by extending their menus and rebranding themselves as Chinees-Indisch , 'Sino-Indonesian'. The addition of Indonesian dishes like nasi goreng (meaty fried rice) to Dutch Chinese restaurant menus made them even more attractive.

Chinese peanut seller

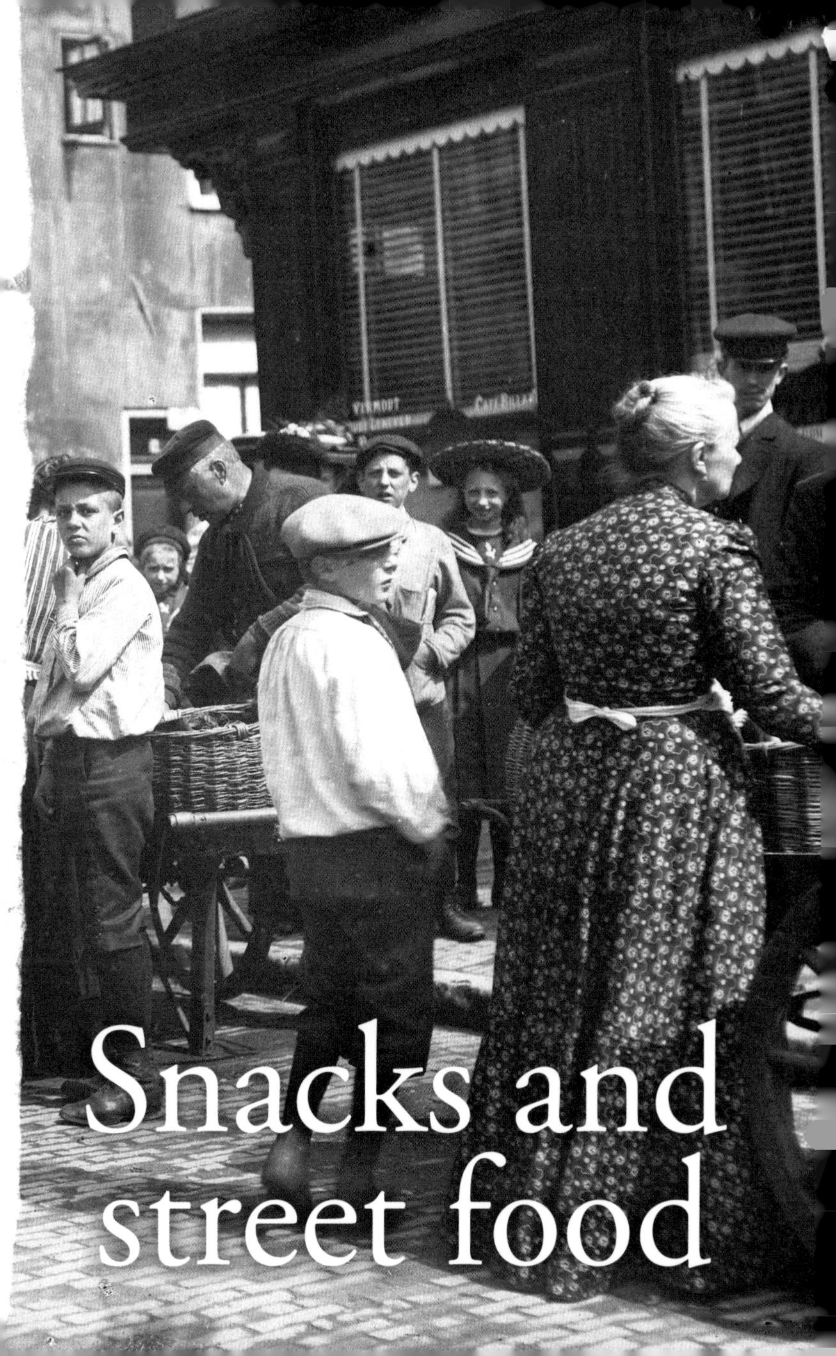

Snacks and street food

HERRING, AMSTERDAM-STYLE

The rest of the Netherlands thinks us weird for it, but we Amsterdammers usually eat our herring [***haring*** - ˈharɪŋ] sliced. Further south, especially in The Hague, Vlaardingen, Scheveningen and Rotterdam, the little fish tends to be grabbed by the tail and gobbled down whole. It's said that the origin of slicing the herring lies in Amsterdam's poverty: you could club together with some mates to order one sliced herring and share it.

Another thing that's unique about how Amsterdam does herring is that it's served with a pickle, laid alongside it on the little cardboard serving tray. There is no culinary reason why herring is traditionally served with diced onions. It is simply that in the days before refrigeration, herrings tasted pretty rancid after a day on the cart. Onions were used to mask the rotting. Now this is no longer necessary, there are herring aficionados who turn their noses up at added onions. They prefer to eat the fish without garnish, or in some cases, with pepper.

Three-quarters of the Dutch prefer to eat their herring right there at the stall. It seems to taste better there than when taken back home. Is that just our imaginations? Actually, no. Our herring expert tells us: 'Herring is nothing other than raw, slightly-spoiled fish with a bit of salt. If you eat up one herring then and there and have the other wrapped to take home, you'll notice that the decomposition has continued and what you eat at home is a different herring.'

For those who like a tipple with their fish, the best accompaniments are *korenwijn* or regular jenever, vodka or aquavit.

To turn it into a meal, partner your herring with a simple potato salad.

◂ ***Previous page:*** *Street vendors on Rozengracht, c. 1907.*

FOOD FROM A HOLE IN THE WALL

In Belgium, wall-mounted vending machines sell bread; in Japan, ladies' underwear or men's ties; in Italy, pizzas; in Moscow, caviar; in China, crab. In the Netherlands, they dispense *kroket* and other fried delicacies.

Dutch Wikipedia describes the *automatiek* in fairly dry terms: 'An *automatiek* is a vending machine. It contains prepared food on a napkin or cardboard serving tray behind glass compartment doors, where it is kept warm. The consumer can open one of these doors after inserting coins and thus remove the product.' Not exactly a romantic description.

Although the food vending machine was not invented in the Netherlands (the first ones appeared in Germany), it became hugely popular in the Netherlands after the Second World War and has remained so ever since. There is an Amsterdam twist to this, as to so much else. The biggest and most famous chain operator of vending machines is Febo (originally the name of a bakery). The name derives from an acronym, Ferdinand Bolstraat, the name of the Amsterdam street on which Febo first had its store. Later, the store moved elsewhere but the name stuck. The first Febo vending machine was opened in 1960 and the rest is history. In fact, by the Sixties, the vending machine was already popular on Dutch shopping streets.

The *kroket* is an Amsterdam invention *par excellence*, because it was the famed pastry cook Herman Kwekkeboom who came up with it; his beef croquettes are still renowned today. Other big names in Dutch *kroket* sales are Van Dobben (originally a sandwich shop) and Holtkamp, who still insist on the original French spelling, *croquette*.

'Diagonal pull', as the Dutch dubbed it, became a common way to round off a night on the town: the doors opened from top left to bottom right, or top right to bottom left, and the homeward-bound revellers could satisfy their bellies.

kalfsvleeskroket
feboburger
FEBO de lekkerste
FEBO de lekkerste..!
FEBO
FEBO

WINTER TOASTED SANDWICH WITH HEMA SMOKED SAUSAGE

Wintertosti met HEMA-worst

['wɪntər 'tɔsti mɛt hema wɔrst]

Makes 2

HEMA, a chain selling household goods and clothes, opened its first store in 1926. From the earliest days, the concept involved cut prices: everything cost a quarter or 50 cents. Two years later, the store added items costing ten cents, 75 cents and a guilder. The smoked sausage for which HEMA is so renowned was 'invented' by chance at the Nieuwendijk branch in 1936. The franchise holder there had purchased too many sausages and got rid of them by selling them hot to shoppers, making a virtue out of necessity. Although HEMA smoked sausage, like herring, is something that the Dutch will always tell you tastes best on the street, it can of course just as well be enjoyed at home.

Ingredients

For the toasted sandwich:

4 slices bread of your choice
4 tbsp mustard of your choice
4 slices bacon or ontbijtspek, baked crispy
6 slices mature farm cheese
½ HEMA smoked sausage, soaked in warm (not boiling) water for 20 minutes and then sliced
1 spring onion, cut into rings
2 tbsp margarine or butter

For the sauce:

2 tbsp curry sauce
2 tbsp mustard

Spread mustard on the slices of bread.
Cover the two sandwiches with a slice of bacon, cheese, slices of smoked sausage, spring onion rings and finally another slice of cheese. Stack the other sandwiches on top.
Toast the sandwiches, either in a sandwich toaster or a frying pan, with a knob of butter.
Meanwhile, make the sauce, for which you mix curry sauce and mustard together, and serve it with the toasted sandwiches.

AMSTERDAM CULINARY TERMS

Amsterdammertje [amstər'damərcə]
1. Straight (vase-like) beer glass holding approx. 30 cl
2. Last drink drained from the bottle
3. A kind of raised *gevulde koek*
4. A traffic bollard
5. A diminutive resident of Amsterdam

Bessie ['bɛsi]: a glass of berry jenever

Blauw [blau] ***(blue)***: drunk

Broodje Mokum ['brocə 'mokəm] ***(Mokum sandwich)***: a white bread sandwich of beef sausage, mature cheese and diced onion

Hachelen ['haxələ(n)]: Yiddish-Dutch for 'to eat'. Je kunt mij de bout hachelen (Why don't you munch on my bout): a self-explanatory imprecation (bout being underworld slang for 'poo')

Jajem ['jajəm]: Yiddish-Dutch jocular term for jenever (taken from the Hebrew for 'wine')

Kachel ['kaxəl]: drunk (probably taken from Hebrew kahol, 'blue', as above)

Keilertje [kɛilərcə]: a small-scale drinks party

Moesselientje [musəlincə]: a pink cake (from French mousseline)

Nasjen [nascən]: to nosh (from Yiddish)

Pikketanussie ['pɪkətanəsi]: tot of jenever

Rooie rakker ['rojə 'rakər]: berry jenever (original meaning: 'a red rabble-rouser', referring to Communist orators around the turn of the century)

Snaaien ['snajən]: to gobble with great relish (from Yiddish)

Vegetable market at Marnixstraat ▸

F H J SCHILDER
Reckitt's
ZAKJE
BLAUW.

Nederlandsche Veiling
AMSTERDAM
A.G.V.
1941 F.1,
A.G.V.
1941 F.1,
AMSTERDAM
AMSTERDAM
A.G.V
1941 F.1,
A.G.V

Cntral Market Hall in Amsterdam, 1941

Acknowledgements

pp. 4-5 'Making do with little': based on *Wat schafte de pot*, article by Peter-Paul de Baar, onsamsterdam.nl, November-December 2005 issue; p. 8 'Rye bread, white bread, brown bread': based on the article *Wit of bruin*, onsamsterdam.nl, November-December 2005 issue; p. 11: *Stratenmakertje* recipe: Koopmans; p. 18: 'Miss Wannée and the *Amsterdamsche Huishoudschool* Cookbook': based on an entry by Floor Meijer in *Digitaal Vrouwenlexicon van Nederland*; p. 25: Lentil recipe: Albert Heijn (AH), *Allerhande* recipe collection; p. 27: Stew recipe: Groenteboer Marco (grocers), Amsterdam, groenteboermarco.nl; p. 34: Onion recipe: Freddie Janssen, *Pickled. Meer dan 60 inspirerende recepten voor pickles, kimchi, azijn en meer*, Veltman Uitgevers; p. 36 recipe Making beef sausage: Ferry Wijsman, nice@ferrywijsman.nl; p. 37 recipe Amsterdam carpaccio: Yvette Jaarsma, curls-culinair.nl; p. 46: *Koggetjes* recipe: bakkersinbedrijf.nl; p. 50: Pancake recipe: Marianne Elfrink, personalfoodcoaching.nl; p. 52: Gingerbread recipe: *Fin de siècle patisserie Recepten van het huis* F.W. Köttelbrink, Het Patrys 2015; p. 54: 'Beer, wine and jenever': based on Niels Wisman, *Een pikketanussie ging er altijd al in*, www.onsamsterdam.nl, November-December 2007 issue, and Maarten Hell, *De herbergdichtheid van Amsterdam*, maartenhell.wordpress.com, November 2012 issue; p. 61: Pick-me-up recipe: AH Allerhande; p. 63: Cocktail recipe: Tess Posthumus, gall.nl/ontdek/cocktails/tess-posthumus; p. 66: 'Binnen Bantammerstraat': based on *Chinezen van Amsterdam* (Huub Sanders, ISG) and Karin Meeuwse, *100 jaar Chinatown*, onsamsterdam.nl, April 2011; p. 73: Sausage toastie recipe: Jacqueline Sluiter, foodblabla.nl.
A great site to find inspiration is www.mokum.nl

Illustrations

babyuka|shutterstock.com; cover; Stadsarchief Amsterdam: 6/7, 20/21, 31, 32/33, 39, 41, 53, 67, 68/69, 77, 78/79; Collectie Archief Bureau Monumentenzorg: 9, 13; Rijksstudio/Rijksmuseum Amsterdam: 15, 51; P.H. Louw at Dutch Wikipedia: 7; Marcel Mulder: 19; freeskyline|shutterstock.com 29; Sylvie Taylor 42,43; , Johannes Walter, naar Johan Braakensiek 55; Instituut voor Sociale Geschiedenis 65; Danilova Janna|Shuttersstock.com 71; Alix Guillard 73; Jacqueline Sluijter 75;

This book is published by Uitgeverij Het Zwarte Schaap.
www.uitgeverijhetzwarteschaap.nl
www.facebook.com/uitgeverijhetzwarteschaap/

Second edition, 2019
ISBN 978 90 823475 9 3
NUR 442

Production: Karen Groeneveld
Design: Repro Design, Deventer